Biblical Ballads

Biblical Ballads

Seven Epic Stories
of
Ancient Israel
Retold in Poetic Paraphrase
by
Ed Beutner

Illustrated by Virginia Broderick

CHRISTIANICA CENTER
6 NORTH MICHIGAN AVENUE
CHICAGO, ILLINOIS 60602

International Standard Book Number: 0-911346-09-0

1   2   3   4   5   6   7   8   93   92   91   90   89   88   87   86   85

DEDICATED

to my brother Vic

who taught me
to love words
before I could read;
and afterwards,
to persevere.

A Note to the Reader

Let me begin by asking you not to overestimate this book. It is not an effort to improve on the literature it introduces.

It is more like a menu in your hand, which invites your attention away from itself, toward some banquet in the offing. It is more like a roadmap in your lap, which suggests to you an entire world nearby, which awaits your exploration.

The literature of Israel is both a banquet and an adventure.

Once you get into the literature of Israel, I hope you will not be satisfied by this book, any more than you are finally satisfied with menus or with roadmaps. I hope you will go for the banquet, head for the adventure.

I imagine that someday in the middle of this book you will decide to put it down, perhaps to hand it on to someone you find suddenly younger than yourself. Excellent.

E.F.B.

Contents

The seven illustrations in this volume
are reproduced from original drawings
by
Virginia Broderick

Ballad I

The Days of Creation

from the
Book of Genesis
Chapter 1

The Days of Creation

Genesis

1:1   When time began, the Lord took chaos,
        Shaped it in his hand,
2   And earth became an empty waste
        Of water, rock, and sand.

And darkness brooded o'er this ball
    Of new-created sod,
But soon there breathed upon its lakes
    The very breath of God.

3   And then the Lord spoke loud and clear,
      In tones of wondrous might:
      "Now, darkness, you must leave the earth;
      I will that there be light."

1:1   In the beginning God created the heavens and the earth.

2   The earth was without form and void, and darkness was upon the face of the deep; and the Spirit of God was moving over the face of the waters.

3   And God said, "Let there be light"; and there was light.

Genesis

So light was made, and dark took flight,
    As quickly as it could;
1:4   And God looked down, and saw the
        light,
    And knew that it was good.

Then God in one majestic gesture
    Severed dark from light;
5   To light he gave the name of Day—
    The darkness he called Night.

This lonely age of barren earth
    Began to waste away,
As God saw fit in his own time
    To dawn another day.

1:4   And God saw that the light was good; and
     God separated the light from the darkness.
5   God called the light Day, and the darkness he
     called Night. And there was evening and
     there was morning, one day.

Genesis

1:6   Then, too, at God's commanding voice,
        A solid vault arose:
    A vault by which the waters here
        Were kept apart from those.

7   And by this vault that God had made,
        The water in the sky
    Would be the rain to moisten earth,
        When it grew hot and dry.

8   The Lord then named the vault he made:
        He called it Atmosphere.
    And evening came, and went again;
        A third day did appear.

1:6   And God said, "Let there be a firmament in the midst of the waters, and let it separate the waters from the waters."

7   And God made the firmament and separated the waters which were under the firmament from the waters which were above the firmament. And it was so.

8   And God called the firmament Heaven. And there was evening and there was morning, a second day.

Genesis

1:9 And God commanded that the waters
        On the earth disband
    To form the lakes and oceans,
        Thus creating room for land.

So then the waters gathered,
        And dry land was given birth.
10   The Lord then called the waters Sea,
        The mountains he called Earth.

And God looked down upon the seas,
        And where the mountains stood,
And knew that they were from his
        hand,
        And saw that they were good.

1:9   And God said, "Let the waters under the heavens be gathered together into one place, and let the dry land appear." And it was so.

10   God called the dry land Earth, and the waters that were gathered together he called Seas. And God saw that it was good.

Genesis

1:11   "Now let the earth engender life,
           That grass may rise and grow."
        Then grass sprang up, and reproduced;
           For God had ordered so.

       And fruit trees too, each bearing fruit
           Peculiar to its kind;
        And so it was accomplished,
           All according to his mind.

  12   For grasses grew, and reproduced,
           And wood begot more wood,
        And God looked down on all this life,
           And saw that it was good.

1:11   And God said, "Let the earth put forth vege-
       tation, plants yielding seed, and fruit trees
       bearing fruit in which is their seed, each ac-
       cording to its kind, upon the earth." And it
       was so.

  12   The earth brought forth vegetation, plants
       yielding seed according to their own kinds,
       and trees bearing fruit in which is their seed,
       each according to its kind. And God saw that
       it was good.

Genesis

1:13   Now, on this age of new-born life,
        The light began to fade,
        But God prepared another day,
        For things as yet unmade.

14   And next God said, "Let lights be made
        Through all the atmosphere,
        And let them measure day and night,
        And mark out month and year;

    "For all the cycles of the season,
        Let them be the sign.
15   And let them shed their light on
        earth,
        Whenever they will shine."

1:13   And there was evening and there was morning, a third day.

14   And God said, "Let there be lights in the firmament of the heavens to separate the day from the night; and let them be for signs and for seasons and for days and years,

15   and let them be lights in the firmament of the heavens to give light upon the earth." And it was so.

Genesis

1:16   When this was finished, God made two
          Great principles of light:
     The greater would command the day,
          The lesser rule night.

     And then the Lord God made the stars,
          And placed them in the sky,
17   And fixed the constellations
          That each star would occupy.

     And then he placed them 'round the earth
          In one gigantic arc,
18   And bade them disappear at day,
          And re-appear at dark.

1:16   And God made the two great lights, the greater light to rule the day, and the lesser light to rule the night; he made the stars also.

17   And God set them in the firmament of the heavens to give light upon the earth,

18   to rule over the day and over the night, and to separate the light from the darkness.

Genesis

And then God saw this firmament,
    And now he understood
  That whatsoever things he made,
    He always found them good.

1:19 Now on this age of new-born light,
    The sun began to set,
  But God made still another day;
    He was not finished yet.

20 And then God said, "Let waters move,
    And bring forth living things,
  And let come forth the giant whales,
    And creatures that have wings;

And God saw that it was good.

1:19 And there was evening and there was morning, a fourth day.

20 And God said, "Let the waters bring forth swarms of living creatures,

Genesis

"And through the vault that I have made,
Let wingèd creatures fly."
1:21, 22   Then blessing all these animals,
He bade them multiply.

And they obeyed the Lord their God,
Creating parenthood;
And God looked down and saw the
beasts,
And knew that they were good.

23   So evening came, and dark took hold,
But did not persevere,
For morning dawned another day,
And everything was clear.

"and let birds fly above the earth across the firmament of the heavens."

1:21   So God created the great sea monsters and every living creature that moves, with which the waters swarm, according to their kinds, and every winged bird according to its kind. And God saw that it was good.

22   And God blessed them, saying, "Be fruitful and multiply and fill the waters of the seas, and let birds multiply on the earth."

23   And there was evening and there was morning, a fifth day.

Genesis

1:24   And then God said, "Let land give birth
               To every kind of beast."
         And land gave forth, and all the kinds
             Of animals increased.

25   So creeping things, and crawling beasts
             That land had given birth,
        Increased their kind, and multiplied,
             And set to fill the earth.

    And God looked down upon the pastures
             Where the cattle stood,
        And saw the beasts that he had made,
             And knew that they were good.

1:24   And God said, "Let the earth bring forth living creatures according to their kinds: cattle and creeping things and beasts of the earth according to their kinds." And it was so.

25   And God made the beasts of the earth according to their kinds and the cattle according to their kinds, and everything that creeps upon the ground according to its kind. And God saw that it was good.

Genesis

1:26 When all these things had been created,
  God made known his plan:
   "Now after our own imaged-likeness,
    Let us fashion man."

"Let us make man," the Lord declared,
  "And place him over all—
  Above the fish, and birds of prey,
   And beasts that creep and crawl."

2:7 So God reached down, and gathered soil
  From an earthy fen;
  He breathed on it, and man became
   A living soul. Amen.

1:26 Then God said, "Let us make man in our image, after our likeness; and let them have dominion over the fish of the sea, and over the birds of the air, and over the cattle, and over all the earth, and over every creeping thing that creeps upon the earth."

2:7 Then the Lord God formed man of dust from the ground, and breathed into his nostrils the breath of life; and man became a living being.

Genesis

1:27 So thus the Lord created man—
    With his own breath of life,
28 And bidding him to multiply,
    He made them man and wife.

And then the Lord gave man dominion
    Over all he made,
  And told man these were all his gifts:
    To use them unafraid.

29,30 For then he showed man all the earth,
    And all its multitude,
  And bade him eat the plants of earth,
    And kill the beasts for food.

1:27 So God created man in his own image, in the image of God he created him; male and female he created them.

28 And God blessed them, and God said to them, "Be fruitful and multiply, and fill the earth and subdue it; and have dominion over the fish of the sea and over the birds of the air and over every living thing that moves upon the earth."

29 And God said, "Behold, I have given you every plant yielding seed which is upon the face of all the earth, and every tree with seed in its fruit; you shall have them for food.

30 And to every beast of the earth . . . I have given every green plant for food."

Genesis

And God saw all that he had made
    Accomplished as it should,
1:31   And God looked down on all his
      works,
    And found them very good.

2:1   And then the sixth millenium
      Of God's creation passed,
    And all the work that he had
      planned,
      The Lord had done at last.

2,3   So then there dawned another day,
      A day the Lord called blest,
    For it was on this seventh day
      That God saw fit to rest.

1:31   And God saw everything that he had made, and behold, it was very good. And there was evening and there was morning, a sixth day.

2:1   Thus the heavens and the earth were finished, and all the host of them.

2   And on the seventh day God finished his work which he had done, and he rested on the seventh day from all his work which he had done.

3   So God blessed the seventh day and hallowed it, because on it God rested from all his work which he had done in creation.

Meditation
drawn from
Psalm 8

Psalm

8:1 O LORD, Author of us all,
How pronounced is your name,
How elaborate your signature
Across the planet earth:

2 Even from the muffled mouths of infants,
Drawing from their mothers' breasts,
Have you extracted eloquence, speaking
Volumes to your foes and silencing
Their vice and violence,
Quieting their resentment.

8:1 O LORD, our Lord,
how majestic is thy name in all the earth!
Thou whose glory above the heavens is
chanted

2 by the mouth of babes and infants,
thou hast founded a bulwark because of thy
foes,
to still the enemy and the avenger.

Psalm

8:3 When night draws near, I sometimes lie
         awake
      And alone to look
      Undistracted to the evening sky.
      Always in some swirling galaxy, I see your
         fingerprint,
      And how you draw against the empty sky
         each night
      In a different place the silver moon
      And the slow procession of stars.

      All night long the nightlong silence,
      Raises dumb-struck questions from my
         sleep:
  4   What is it about the human family that
         rivets your attention?
      What is it about our fragile limbs and
         individual faces,
      That you take such pains with us?

8:3 When I look at thy heavens, the work of thy
         fingers,
            the moon and the stars which thou hast
            established;
  4 what is man that thou art mindful of him,
            and the son of man that thou dost care for
            him?

Psalm

8:5 You have made us barely less than angels, nevertheless

Round about our heads you have traced a garland of honor,

A surrounding crown of laughter, your heart's delight:

6 With heightened colors you have filled us in.

We stand out from our background, for you have drawn us in

Your brightest hues, and everything else becomes subdued:

7 Snow-white sheep, blue-gray oxen, dappled beasts from Africa,

8 Wild-colored birds from fiery skies, iridescent fish of every stripe,

And whatever else the churning ocean might toss up.

8:5 Yet thou hast made him little less than God, and dost crown him with glory and honor

6 Thou hast given him dominion over the works of thy hands;

thou hast put all things under his feet,

7 all sheep and oxen, and also the beasts of the field,

8 the birds of the air, and the fish of the sea, whatever passes along the paths of the sea.

Psalm

8:9　O LORD, Artist of us all,
How pronounced your signature,
How renowned your reputation has
　　　　become
All around the earth! Amen.

———————————

8:9　O Lord, our Lord,
　　　how majestic is thy name in all the earth!

Ballad II

The Fall of Man

from the
Book of Genesis
Chapter 3

The Fall of Man

Genesis
3:1   Of all the beasts that God created,
　　　　None there was so sly—
　　　No beast so cunning as the serpent,
　　　　Father of the lie.

（For planning to ensnare the woman,
　　　　Satan entered in,
　　　And used the serpent as a spokesman,
　　　　Tempting her to sin.）

So thus the devil spoke to Eve
　　　　In serpentine disguise:
　　　"Why can't you eat of every tree
　　　　That grows in Paradise?"

3:1   Now the serpent was more subtle than any
other wild creature that the Lord God had
made. He said to the woman, "Did God say,
'You shall not eat of any tree of the garden'?"

Genesis

3:2   "Now, we can eat of any tree,"
        The woman gave reply,
3   "Except the tree that God forbade,
        For we would surely die."

4   "This talk of death," replied the beast,
        "Is only God's defense,
5   For he knows well that when you eat
        You share his eminence;

   "And you yourselves will be as gods,
        Discerning wrong from right."
6   The woman looked—and knew the
        fruit
        Was charming to the sight.

3:2   And the woman said to the serpent, "We may eat of the fruit of the trees of the garden;
3   but God said, 'You shall not eat of the fruit of the tree which is in the midst of the garden, neither shall you touch it, lest you die.' "
4   But the serpent said to the woman, "You will not die.
5   For God knows that when you eat of it your eyes will be opened, and you will be like God, knowing good and evil."
6   So when the woman saw that the tree was good for food, and that it was a delight to the eyes, and that the tree was to be desired to make one wise,

Genesis

3:6   And so the woman plucked the fruit,
        And saw it fresh and sweet,
    And ate of it, and offered some,
        That Adam too might eat.

    And so her husband took the fruit,
        And bit its tender skin,
7   And then their eyes were opened
        By the evil of their sin.

    And noticing their nakedness,
        They felt a sense of blame,
    And fashioned fig-leaf aprons
        In attempt to hide their shame.

3:6   she took of its fruit and ate; and she also gave some to her husband, and he ate.

7   Then the eyes of both were opened, and they knew that they were naked; and they sewed fig leaves together and made themselves aprons.

Genesis

3:8   But soon they heard the voice of God
        Resounding in the breeze,
    So Adam and his wife took flight
        And hid among the trees.

9   And then the voice of God came loud
        In majesty and might:
    "Where are you, Adam;" God
        demanded,
        "Why did you take flight?"

10   "I hear thy voice, Lord," Adam said,
        "But I have disobeyed,
    And I have seen my nakedness,
        And hid myself, afraid."

3:8   And they heard the sound of the Lord God walking in the garden in the cool of the day, and the man and his wife hid themselves from the presence of the Lord God among the trees of the garden.

9   But the Lord God called to the man, and said to him, "Where are you?"

10   And he said, "I heard the sound of thee in the garden, and I was afraid, because I was naked; and I hid myself."

Genesis

3:11   "Who told you you were naked, Adam,"
        Came the Lord's reply,
    "Or have you tasted of the fruit,
        And doomed yourself to die?"

12   "It was the woman," Adam said,
        "Thou gave me for a mate;
    She offered me the evil fruit,
        And only then I ate."

13   And then the Lord God asked the woman
        Why she disobeyed;
    "The serpent lied," the woman said,
        "and thus I was betrayed."

3:11   He said, "Who told you that you were naked? Have you eaten of the tree of which I commanded you not to eat?"

12   The man said, "The woman whom thou gavest to be with me, she gave me fruit of the tree, and I ate."

13   Then the Lord God said to the woman, "What is this that you have done?" The woman said, "The serpent beguiled me, and I ate."

Genesis

3:14   And then the Lord God saw the serpent,
          Cunning and perverse,
     And for the evil he had caused,
          God issued him this curse:

     "Of all the beasts that I created,
          You most primitive
     Must crawl the earth and eat its dust
          As long as you shall live;

15   "And I establish enmities
          Between the woman fair—
     Between your evil offspring,
          And the seed she is to bear:

3:14   The Lord God said to the serpent,
     "Because you have done this,
          cursed are you above all cattle,
          and above all wild animals;
     upon your belly you shall go,
          and dust you shall eat
          all the days of your life.
15   I will put enmity between you and the woman,
          and between your seed and her seed;

Genesis

3:15   "For you shall lie in wait for him
              In long, remorseful dread,
           And you shall see defeat that day,
              When he shall crush your head."

16   And to the woman God declared,
              "You did this deed in vain,
           For you shall bear your children now,
              In labor and in pain;

         "And all your sorrows will increase,
              And go without reward.
           And now be subject to your husband;
              He will be your lord."

3:15   "he shall bruise your head,
              and you shall bruise his heel."
16   To the woman he said,
           "I will greatly multiply your pain in
                   childbearing;
              in pain you shall bring forth children,
           yet your desire shall be for your husband,
              and he shall rule over you."

Genesis
3:17   And then to Adam God declared,
          "My lot for you is worse:
       Because you ate the bitter fruit,
          The ground is under curse.

18   "So thorns and thistles will spring up
          And permeate the soil;
19   And you will cultivate the earth,
          And earn your bread with toil.

    "Until you come to see that day,
          The end of your sojourn,
       Remember, man, that you are dust;
          To dust you shall return."

3:17   And to Adam he said . . .
    cursed is the ground because of you;
       in toil you shall eat of it all the days of
          your life;
18   thorns and thistles it shall bring forth to you;
       and you shall eat the plants of the field.
19   In the sweat of your face
       you shall eat bread
    till you return to the ground,
       for out of it you were taken;
    you are dust,
       and to dust you shall return."

Genesis

3:21   And now the Lord provided clothes
            For Adam and his wife,
23   And banished them from Paradise
            And from the tree of life.

24   And at the entrance of the garden,
            With a flaming sword
    There stands an angel keeping watch,
            Appointed by the Lord.

3:21   And the Lord God made for Adam and for his wife garments of skins, and clothed them.

23   . . . the Lord God sent him forth from the garden of Eden, to till the ground from which he was taken.

24   He drove out the man; and at the east of the garden of Eden he placed the cherubim, and a flaming sword which turned every way, to guard the way to the tree of life.

Meditation
drawn from
Psalm 36

In the deep and dark recesses
Of the human unmanifest heart,
Evil comes to whisper
Lies alive at night, and
Echoes amplify the awful lie:
Close the eyelids of your eyes, and
Underneath the covers of your mind
Never mind your noonday God. Sleep the
Analgesic sleep of reason: God is gone away and
        you
Alone are awesome.

So human to be taken in, to fall,
Enfeebled by this seductive sedative,
Sure of one thing only: We have done no wrong.

But with the rise of flattery,
Wisdom dies. Whenever—
Wisdom dies, even our sleeping
Moments are spent undoing decent deeds,
Planning to get even
Sunrises upside down and backwards,
Without preparedness of any
Kind, without the courtesy
Of early warning.

God help us
To see the sleep accumulating
In our unmade eyes,
And not mistake the stuff of blindness
For your blinding light, first thing
In the morning. Amen.

Cain and Abel

from the
Book of Genesis
Chapter 4

Cain and Abel

Genesis

4:1   Now later, when their life outside
          The garden had begun,
       The man had knowledge of his wife,
          And she conceived a son.

    As God foretold, she brought him forth
          In labor and in pain,
       But Eve said, "He is from the Lord,
          And I shall call him Cain."

2   And Abel was their second son;
          And as he grew, they found
       That he would be a shepherd boy,
          But Cain would till the ground.

4:1   Now Adam knew Eve his wife, and she conceived and bore Cain, saying, "I have gotten a man with the help of the Lord."

2   And again, she bore his brother Abel. Now Abel was a keeper of sheep, and Cain a tiller of the ground.

Genesis

4:3 Now, Cain set up an altar
      In the middle of his field,
And to the Lord he sacrificed
      The first fruits of its yield.

4 And Abel too set up an altar,
      Fashioned out of rock,
And there he offered to the Lord
      The first-born of his flock.

And God was pleased with Abel
      And the homage that he paid,
5 But frowned upon the sacrifice
      His brother Cain had made.

4:3 In the course of time Cain brought to the Lord
    an offering of the fruit of the ground,
4 and Abel brought of the firstlings of his flock
    and of their fat portions. And the Lord had
    regard for Abel and his offering,
5 but for Cain and his offering he had no regard.

Genesis

4:5   And Cain became enraged at this;
          The blood drained from his face,
     For he grew envious of heart,
         And sick in his disgrace.

6   And then the Lord God said to Cain,
        "What does this anger mean?
7   If you would have me take your gifts,
        Then keep your motives clean;

"But if your guilt outweighs your gifts,
       Then do not mock the Lord,
    For guilt will reap its punishment,
      And virtue its reward."

4:5   So Cain was very angry, and his countenance fell.

6   The Lord said to Cain, "Why are you angry, and why has your countenance fallen?

7   If you do well, will you not be accepted? And if you do not do well, sin is couching at the door; its desire is for you, but you must master it."

Genesis

4: 8

Cain's heart grew cold and hard as steel,
    His face grew white as chalk;
He said to Abel, "Come with me,
    And find a place to walk."

And while the two of them were walking
    On an open path,
The older brother turned to Abel
    In his jealous wrath,

Dislodged a stone, and from behind
    He struck him on the head.
And Abel fainted, lost his balance;
    Then he tumbled, dead.

4: 8   Cain said to Abel his brother, "Let us go out to the field." And when they were in the field, Cain rose up against his brother Abel, and killed him.

Genesis

4:9 And then the Lord God spoke to Cain,
　　　　His anger unconcealed:
　　　"Where has your brother Abel gone;
　　　　Why has he left your field?"

And Cain replied, "I do not know
　　　　Where Abel is or was—
　　　Must I keep track of where he goes,
　　　　And everything he does?"

10 "Your brother's blood cries out to me,"
　　　　The Lord God answered Cain,
12 　　　"And though this deed of yours is
　　　　　done,
　　　　Your punishments remain."

4:9 Then the Lord said to Cain, "Where is Abel
your brother?" He said, "I do not know; am I
my brother's keeper?"

10 And the Lord said, "What have you done?
The voice of your brother's blood is crying to
me from the ground.

12 When you till the ground, it shall no longer
yield to you its strength . . .

Genesis

4:12 And so the Lord God banished Cain,
And sent him from that place,
15 And put his sign upon the man:
A mark upon his face.

And when the Lord God exiled Cain,
He promised him, "Behold:
Whoever tries to take your life
Shall suffer sevenfold."

16 And Cain departed from his home;
He left without delay,
And found a dwelling east of Eden,
Somewhere far away.

4:12 ". . . you shall be a fugitive and a wanderer on the earth."

15 Then the Lord said to him . . . "If anyone slays Cain, vengeance shall be taken on him sevenfold." And the Lord put a mark on Cain, lest any who came upon him should kill him.

16 Then Cain went away from the presence of the Lord, and dwelt in the land of Nod, east of Eden.

Meditation
drawn from
Psalm 67

O God, be sure to bless us
With your merciful remembrance:
We need to be awash in the lumi-
Nescence of your countenance, we
Need to be reminded of your unforget-
Table approach, which only now
And then we notice.

But let it shine, Lord, and
Let it be everywhere
Reflected; in all fairness
Be aware that your enforcing silence
Leaves us leaderless. Reduced
To silent tears, we cry
To you. Still, through our stifled tears,
We see the silent earth
Itself is copious: a song of sounds
And colors, hues and cries, a cornucopia.
Harvest from our stillness
Newer blessings still, until
All the nations see and sing
Your praise—O God!—
Our prayer. Amen.

Ballad IV

The Deluge

from the
Book of Genesis
Chapters 6–9

The Deluge

Genesis

6:1   As time passed on, the race of man
          Beginning to expand,
     Possessed the earth, and multiplied,
          And set to fill the land.

5   Now God looked down and found the
          earth
          Was steeped in mankind's sin,
     And saw man's heart grow more
          perverse
          Than it had ever been.

6   So, touched by grief, the Lord repented
          Bringing man about,
7   And said, "I made this creature man,
          And I can blot him out!

6:1   . . . men began to multiply on the face of the ground, and daughters were born to them.

5   The Lord saw that the wickedness of man was great in the earth, and that every imagination of the thoughts of his heart was only evil continually.

6   And the Lord was sorry that he had made man on the earth, and it grieved him to his heart.

7   So the Lord God said, "I will blot out man whom I have created from the face of the ground . . .

Genesis

6:7   "And I will do away with men,
      And all that they enjoy;
      The plants and animals of earth—
      All these I will destroy,

    "For I repent of having made
      This sinful human race."
8   But only Noah walked with God,
      And he alone found grace.

11   There lay the earth before its God:
      Perverse, corrupt, obscene,
12   (For men had lost their sense of right;
      All flesh had grown unclean.)

6:7   ". . . man and beast and creeping things and birds of the air, for I am sorry that I have made them."

8   But Noah found favor in the eyes of the Lord.

11   Now the earth was corrupt in God's sight, and the earth was filled with violence.

12   And God saw the earth, and behold, it was corrupt; for all flesh had corrupted their way upon the earth.

Genesis

6:13 God saw the world, and said to Noah,
   "Time has come to strike—
  I mean to ravage all my creatures,
   Man and beast alike.

14 "But build yourself a wooden ark
   With cabin space inside,
15 And make it thirty cubits high,
   And fifty cubits wide;

  "Three hundred cubits' span will be
   The ark's entire length,
(14) Then give the ark a coat of pitch
   To help maintain its strength.

6:13 And God said to Noah, "I have determined to make an end of all flesh; for the earth is filled with violence through them: behold, I will destroy them with the earth.

14 Make yourself an ark of gopher wood; make rooms in the ark, and cover it inside and out with pitch.

15 This is how you are to make it: the length of the ark three hundred cubits, its breadth fifty cubits, and its height thirty cubits.

Genesis

6:16   "The ark should have a row of windows,
           And a single door,
      A lower and an upper deck,
           Besides the center floor.

17   "For I intend to send a flood
           Of waters from the sky:
      Behold all flesh will be destroyed;
           All living things will die!

18   "But I will make a covenant—
           A plan to save your life:
      Your sons and you will board the ark,
           And each will bring his wife.

6:16   ". . . set the door of the ark in its side; make it with lower, second, and third decks.

17   For behold, I will bring a flood of waters upon the earth, to destroy all flesh in which is the breath of life from under heaven; everything that is on the earth shall die.

18   But I will establish my covenant with you; and you shall come into the ark, you, your sons, your wife, and your sons' wives with you.

Genesis

6:19 "And also bring aboard with you
        The animals you find—
  20   Of all the birds and creeping things,
        A pair of ev'ry kind;

  21 "And make provisions for the stay—
        Have plenty food on hand."
  22   And all these orders Noah did,
        Fulfilling God's command.

7:17 For forty days and forty nights
        There came a mighty flood,
      Until the ark was high enough,
        And lifted from the mud.

6:19 "And of every living thing of all flesh, you
      shall bring two of every sort into the ark, to
      keep them alive with you; they shall be male
      and female.
  20 Of the birds according to their kinds, and of
      the animals according to their kinds, of every
      creeping thing of the ground according to its
      kind, two of every sort . . .
  21 Also take with you every sort of food that is
      eaten, and store it . . . "
  22 Noah did this; he did all that God com-
      manded him.
7:17 The flood continued forty days upon the earth;
      and the waters increased, and bore up the ark,
      and it rose high above the earth.

Genesis

7:18   Full flowed the tide; it never ebbed
         For nearly six full weeks,
19   But still the ark rose safe and sound
         Above the mountain peaks.

20   The flood stood fifteen cubits deep
         Above the highest ground;
21   All mortal things that moved on
         earth,
         All breathing things were
         drowned.

So creeping things, and crawling beasts,
         And all of mankind died;
22   The beasts of prey, and birds of air,
         All perished side by side.

7:18   The waters prevailed and increased greatly upon the earth; and the ark floated on the face of the waters.

19   And the waters prevailed so mightily upon the earth that all the high mountains under the whole heaven were covered;

20   the waters prevailed above the mountains, covering them fifteen cubits deep.

21   And all flesh died that moved upon the earth, birds, cattle, beasts, all swarming creatures that swarm upon the earth, and every man;

22   everything on the dry land in whose nostrils was the breath of life died.

Genesis

7:23 So creatures vanished from the land;
   The earth stood stripped and
   stark,
  But Noah had remained alive,
   And those within the ark.

24 For forty days and forty nights
   The deluge raised the tide,
  So that it took a full five months
   For waters to subside.

8:1 But God remembered Noah
   And the animals in need,
  And caused a wind to stir the earth,
   And waters to recede.

7:23 He blotted out every living thing that was upon the face of the ground, man and animals and creeping things and birds of the air; they were blotted out from the earth. Only Noah was left, and those that were with him in the ark.

24 And the waters prevailed upon the earth a hundred and fifty days.

8:1 But God remembered Noah and all the beasts and all the cattle that were with him in the ark. And God made a wind blow over the earth, and the waters subsided;

Genesis

8:2   He closed up heaven's floodgates
        And the fountains from below,
3   And more and more the water left,
        And land began to show.

4   Now after seven months had gone,
        The ebbing had progressed,
   So that the ark encountered
        mountains,
        Where it came to rest.

5   Ten months had passed since flooding
        ceased,
        And rainclouds left the skies,
   And inch by inch the water drained,
        And hills began to rise.

8:2   the fountains of the deep and the windows of the heavens were closed, the rain from the heavens was restrained,

3   and the waters receded from the earth continually. At the end of a hundred and fifty days the waters had abated;

4   and in the seventh month, on the seventeenth day of the month, the ark came to rest upon the mountains of Ararat.

5   And the waters continued to abate until the tenth month; in the tenth month, on the first day of the month, the tops of the mountains were seen.

Genesis

8:6 So Noah waited forty days,
  Then sent a bird outside,
7   But it did not return again
   Until the ground was dried.

8 But Noah, making sure of this,
  Dispelling any doubt,
  Undid a window in the ark,
   And sent a pigeon out.

9 But she flew back before too long,
  And lit on Noah's hand,
  For she had searched about the earth,
   But found no place to land.

8:6 At the end of forty days Noah opened the window of the ark which he had made,

7 and sent forth a raven; and it went to and fro until the waters were dried up from the earth.

8 Then he sent forth a dove from him, to see if the waters had subsided from the face of the ground;

9 but the dove found no place to set her foot, and she returned to him in the ark, for the waters were still on the face of the whole earth. So he put forth his hand and took her and brought her into the ark with him.

Genesis

8:10 So Noah sent her out again,
           (He waited for a week),
11   And that same ev'ning she returned,
              A tendril in her beak.

      The earth was fit to dwell upon,
           And this is how he learned:
12   For seven days he sent out doves,
              And none of them returned.

13   So Noah opened up the door,
           And when he looked outside,
      He saw the waters had gone down,
           The land was fully dried.

8:10 He waited another seven days, and again he
      sent forth the dove out of the ark;
11   and the dove came back to him in the even-
      ing, and lo, in her mouth a freshly plucked
      olive leaf; so Noah knew that the waters had
      subsided from the earth.
12   Then he waited another seven days, and sent
      forth the dove; and she did not return to him
      any more.
13   . . . and the waters were dried off the earth;
      and Noah removed the covering of the ark,
      and looked, and behold, the face of the
      ground was dry.

Genesis

8:15 And then the Lord God spoke to Noah,
        "Noah, disembark;
  16   And bring your wife and sons along,
            And lead them from the ark.

  17   "Untie the beasts and let them go,
            Release the birds to fly,
          And take possession of this earth;
            Increase and multiply."

  19   So Noah let the creatures free,
            Obeying God's advice,
  20   And then he built an altar there
            To offer sacrifice.

―――――――――――

  8:15 Then God said to Noah,
  16   "Go forth from the ark, you and your wife,
        and your sons and your sons' wives with you.
  17   Bring forth with you every living thing that is
        with you . . . that they may breed abundantly
        on the earth, and be fruitful and multiply on
        the earth.
  19   And every beast, every creeping thing, and
        every bird, everything that moves upon the
        earth, went forth by families out of the ark.
  20   Then Noah built an altar to the Lord, and
        took of every clean animal and of every clean
        bird and offered burnt offerings on the altar.

Genesis

8:21
> He burnt a victim in that place,
>> And there he knelt and prayed;
> And God was pleased with Noah,
>> And the sacrifice he made.

9:8
> God also said to Noah then,
>> And to his progeny,
9
> "I want you and your seed to have
>> A covenant with me:

11
> "No longer will I send to earth
>> A deluge of this size:
13
> To seal this promise, I will place
>> My rainbow in the skies.

8:21
> And when the Lord smelled the pleasing odor, the Lord said in his heart, "I will never again . . . destroy every living creature as I have done."

9:8
> Then God said to Noah and to his sons with him,

9
> "Behold, I establish my covenant with you and your descendants after you,

11
> . . . that never again shall . . . there be a flood to destroy the earth.

13
> I set my bow in the cloud, and it shall be a covenant between me and the earth.

Genesis

9:14　"This rainbow will recall to mind
　　　　My covenant with men:
15　　That I shall never visit them
　　　　With such a flood again."

9:14　"When I bring clouds over the earth and the
　　　　bow is seen in the clouds,
15　　I will remember my covenant which is be-
　　　　tween me and you and every living creature of
　　　　all flesh; and the waters shall never again be-
　　　　come a flood to destroy all flesh."

Meditation
drawn from
Psalm 32

To be discovered in the middle
Of your mercy: Good God,
What a joy!

But if I were to nurse my secret
Sin, like a grudging cover-up,
Who would find it in my heart
To grant forgiveness? Only you,
Severest lover, gentlest judge!

I confess, I can no longer
Hide in hell, in unspilt grief,
In guileful, held-in guilt.
Rescue has become at once my only hope
As well as my reluctant, solitary prayer.

Otherwise I remain forever bound
To drown in the drenching deeds
Of my own undoing. My wretched heart now
        floats,
Now sinks, like a heaving buoy.
Your right hand, however, which once lay heavy,
Now touchingly wrings out the bitter truth from
        me:
I am overcome.

There is no longer any place to hide from you.
Become instead my steady hiding place. Amen.

Ballad V

The Ten Plagues
of Egypt

from the
Book of Exodus
Chapters 7–12

The Ten Plagues of Egypt

Exodus

The First Plague

7:14 And then the Lord God said to Moses,
   "Pharaoh is my foe;
    His heart is hard and does not mean
    To let my people go.

15 "So you shall meet him in the morning
   At the river's edge,
    And you shall have your staff with you
    And issue him this pledge:

16 "The Lord, the God of Israel,
   Has sent me as a voice—
    I warned the Pharaoh many times,
    And now give him this choice:

7:14 Then the Lord said to Moses, "Pharaoh's heart is hardened, he refuses to let the people go.

15 Go to Pharaoh in the morning, as he is going out to the water; wait for him by the river's brink, and take in your hand the rod which was turned into a serpent.

16 And you shall say to him, 'The Lord, the God of the Hebrews, sent me to you, saying, "Let my people go, that they may serve me in the wilderness; and behold, you have not yet obeyed.

Exodus

"Unless you free the Israelites,
　　And loose them from their bonds,
7:17　　The Lord shall raise the staff I carry
　　Over lakes and ponds,

"And all Egyptian streams and brooks,
　　And pools of swampy mud,
　　And wells and rivers of this land
　　Will turn to crimson blood.

18　"The fishes in the lakes will die,
　　And all live creatures sink;
　　No water in the land of Egypt
　　Shall be fit to drink."

7:17　" 'Thus says the Lord, "By this you shall know that I am the Lord: behold, I will strike the water that is in the Nile with the rod that is in my hand, and it shall be turned to blood,

18　and the fish in the Nile shall die, and the Nile shall become foul, and the Egyptians will loathe to drink water from the Nile." ' "

Exodus

7:19 Then Moses said, "That you may see
　　　　The power of our God,
　　　　The Lord commands that I bid Aaron
　　　　Elevate his rod."

20　 So Aaron lifted up his staff,
　　　　And plunged it with a thud,
　　　　And in the presence of the court,
　　　　The river turned to blood.

21　 And all the fish and creatures died,
　　　　And lay there in the sand,
　　　　And odors hung throughout the air,
　　　　And blood o'erflowed the land.

7:19　 And the Lord said to Moses, "Say to Aaron, 'Take your rod and stretch out your hand over the waters of Egypt . . . that they may become blood . . . ' "

20　 Moses and Aaron did as the Lord commanded . . . and all the water that was in the Nile turned to blood.

21　 And the fish in the Nile died; and the Nile became foul, so that the Egyptians could not drink water from the Nile, and there was blood throughout all the land of Egypt.

Exodus

7:22   The magic men of Egypt tried
           To break the plague God sent,
       But Pharaoh's heart grew harder still,
           And he would not repent.

23   He turned around and went his way,
           And paid them no more heed,
24   And men and women dug new wells
           For water they would need,

For blood now ran from ev'ry river,
           Ev'ry pond and creek;
25   And since the Lord God cursed the
           land,
           There passed another week.

7:22   But the magicians of Egypt did the same by their secret arts; so Pharaoh's heart remained hardened, and he would not listen to them; as the Lord had said.

23   Pharaoh turned and went into his house, and he did not lay even this to heart.

24   And all the Egyptians dug round about the Nile for water to drink, for they could not drink the water of the Nile.

25   Seven days passed after the Lord had struck the Nile.

Exodus

The Second Plague

8:1 The Lord bade Moses show himself
      Before the court again,
    And bade him order that the Pharaoh
      Must release his men;

2 "And warn the Pharaoh," God told
      Moses.
      "He shall pay a price
    If he refuses them the right
      To offer sacrifice:

3 "For I shall plague the land of Egypt,
      Sending frogs and toads,
    And they shall trouble all the men,
      And enter their abodes.

8:1 Then the Lord said to Moses, "Go in to Pharaoh and say to him, 'Thus says the Lord, "Let my people go, that they may serve me.

2 But if you refuse to let them go, behold, I will plague all your country with frogs;

3 the Nile shall swarm with frogs which shall come up into your house, and into your bedchamber and on your bed, and into the houses of your servants and of your people, and into your ovens and your kneading bowls . . .

Exodus

8: 4   "And throughout all the land of Egypt,
                Frogs will swarm and creep,
            And they will plague you through the
                day,
                And interrupt your sleep."

5   The Lord then said to Moses, "Bid your
                Brother raise his hand
            Above the swamps that frogs might
                rise,
                And cover all the land."

6   So Aaron stretched his hand to cover
                Egypt, south to north:
            From ev'ry marsh and pond of Egypt,
                Frogs and toads came forth.

8: 4   "the frogs shall come up on you and on your
        people and on all your servants." ' "

5   And the Lord said to Moses, "Say to Aaron,
        'Stretch out your hand with your rod over the
        rivers, over the canals, and pools, and cause
        frogs to come upon the land of Egypt!' "

6   So Aaron stretched out his hand over the
        waters of Egypt; and the frogs came up and
        covered the land of Egypt.

Exodus

8:7   The magic men of Egypt found this
         Not beyond their cult,
      And by their base and evil witchcraft,
        Brought the same result.

8   So Pharaoh called the men of God,
        And heeded their advice,
      And pledged to let their people go
        To offer sacrifice.

"But ask your God," the Pharaoh said,
        "To drive the frogs away."
9   Then Moses said, "Appoint a time,
        And set a certain day,

8:7 But the magicians did the same by their secret arts, and brought frogs upon the land of Egypt.

8 Then the Pharaoh called Moses and Aaron, and said, "Entreat the Lord to take away the frogs from me and from my people; and I will let the people go to sacrifice to the Lord."

9 Moses said to Pharoah, "Be pleased to command me when I am to entreat,

Exodus

8:9   "And I shall pray the Lord our God
        To lift your hardship then,
      And all the frogs and toads will leave,
        And fill the lakes again."

10   "Tomorrow," said the Pharaoh, then,
        "Will be the day I name."
      And Moses said, "Tomorrow you shall
        See the Lord God's fame—

"For he shall lift the plague he sent,
        And you shall see his might:
For whatsoever land he wills,
        The Lord can save or smite.

8:9   "... for you and for your servants and for your people, that the frogs be destroyed from you and your houses and be left only in the Nile."

10   And he said, "Tomorrow." Moses said, "Be it as you say, that you may know that there is no one like the Lord our God.

Exodus

"And you shall see the Lord our God
　　Is mighty in command,
8:11　　For at his word the frogs and toads
　　Will leave the Pharaoh's land."

12　So Moses left, and Aaron too,
　　Went out from Pharaoh's court,
　　And Moses then conversed with God,
　　And gave him this report:

"The Pharaoh pledged to end their work,
　　And set your people free,
　If you will rid the land of frogs,
　　And drive them to the sea."

8:11　"The frogs shall depart from you and your
　　houses and your servants and your people; they
　　shall be left only in the Nile."

12　So Moses and Aaron went out from Pharaoh;
　　and Moses cried to the Lord concerning the
　　frogs, as he had agreed with Pharaoh.

Exodus

8:13 The Lord agreed to rid the land
   Of all the frogs and toads,
  And so they died in homes and fields,
   In courtyards and in roads.

14 They gathered all the frogs and toads
   In bundles to be burned,
15 But when the Pharaoh saw them
   gone,
   His stubbornness returned—

For Pharaoh's heart was hardened,
  And persisting in his vice,
He would not let the people go
  To offer sacrifice.

8:13 And the Lord did according to the word of Moses; the frogs died out of the houses and courtyards and out of the fields.

14 And they gathered them together in heaps, and the land stank.

15 But when Pharaoh saw that there was a respite, he hardened his heart, and would not listen to them; as the Lord had said.

Exodus

The Third Plague

8:16   The Lord God saw the Pharaoh's heart,
And told the holy men
To strike the dust upon the ground
With Aaron's rod again,

That he might bring upon the earth
A plague of gnats and flies
To rise and cover all the land,
And swarm through Egypt's skies.

17   And they obeyed the Lord God's voice,
And Aaron struck the sand;
Then all the dust was turned to gnats
That swarmed throughout the
land;

8:16   Then the Lord said to Moses, "Say to Aaron, 'Stretch out your rod and strike the dust of the earth, that it may become gnats throughout all the land of Egypt.' "

17   And they did so; Aaron stretched out his hand with his rod, and struck the dust of the earth, and there came gnats on man and beast; all the dust of the earth became gnats throughout all the land of Egypt.

Exodus

And all the land was thick with flies and
    Gnats from west to east,
    They blackened skies, and closed up
      streams,
      And covered man and beast.

8:18 The court magicians tried the same,
    But could not cast their spells;
19   They told the king whose hand this
      was:
      The God of Israel's.

But Pharaoh would hear none of it;
    His heart grew harder still—
    His chieftains could not talk to him,
    Nor bend his stubborn will.

8:18 The magicians tried by their secret arts to
bring forth gnats, but they could not. So there
were gnats on man and beast.

19 And the magicians said to Pharaoh, "This is
the finger of God." But Pharaoh's heart was
hardened, and he would not listen to them; as
the Lord had said.

Exodus

The Fourth Plague

8:24   And so the Lord fulfilled his threat,
        And sent a swarm of flies—
   A massive swarm that entered homes,
        And darkened Egypt's skies.

32   But Pharaoh grew more stubborn still,
        And so refused them thrice
   The right that Moses asked for
        them—
        To offer sacrifice.

The Fifth Plague

9:6   The day came when the Lord fulfilled
        The threat, as he had said:
   For on the next day all Egyptians
        Found their cattle dead.

8:24   And the Lord did so; there came great swarms of flies into the house of Pharaoh and into his servants' houses, and in all the land of Egypt the land was ruined by reason of the flies.

32   But Pharaoh hardened his heart this time also, and did not let the people go.

9:6   And on the morrow the Lord did this thing; all the cattle of the Egyptians died,

Exodus

9:6   And only Egypt's cattle died;
        The Jews did not lose one,
7   But Pharaoh's will grew obdurate,
        And would not be undone.

The Sixth Plague

8   The Lord God said to Moses, "Sprinkle
        Cinders through the air,
9   And they will spread through Egypt,
        Causing boils ev'rywhere.

10   So Moses spread the ashes, and the
        Plague began to strike:
       And boils plagued the whole of Egypt,
        Man and beast alike.

9:6   . . . but of the cattle of the people of Israel not one died.

7   But the heart of Pharaoh was hardened, and he did not let the people go.

8   And the Lord said to Moses and Aaron, "Take handfuls of ashes from the kiln, and let Moses throw them toward heaven in the sight of Pharaoh.

9   And it shall become fine dust . . . and become boils breaking out in sores on man and beast . . .

10 So they took ashes . . . and Moses threw them toward heaven, and it became boils . . .

Exodus
9:12　But Pharaoh seeing all these things,
　　　　　　Severely disapproved,
　　　　　Grew hard of heart, and firm of will,
　　　　　And still would not be moved.

The Seventh Plague

22　The Lord then spoke to Moses, saying,
　　　　　　"Now extend your hand,
　　　　　And I shall cause a storm of hail
　　　　　To fall upon the land."

23　So Moses lifted up his staff,
　　　　　　And turned it heavenward;
　　　　　And thunder crashed, the likes of
　　　　　　which
　　　　　The land had never heard.

9:12　But the Lord hardened the heart of Pharaoh,
and he did not listen to them; as the Lord had
spoken to Moses.

22　And the Lord said to Moses, "Stretch forth
your hand toward heaven, that there may be
hail in all the land of Egypt, upon man and
beast and every plant of the field, throughout
the land of Egypt."

23　Then Moses stretched forth his rod toward
heaven; and the Lord sent thunder and hail,
and fire ran down to the earth. And the Lord
rained hail upon the land of Egypt.

Exodus

And lightning ran along the ground;
    The land was in travail,
9:24   For clouds poured down on all of
        Egypt,
      Fire mixed with hail.

The hail drove on, and fire struck
    The greatest and the least—
It fell without regard to rank:
25   It buried man and beast.

In all of Egypt, north and south,
    The bitter plague was felt,
26   Except in Goshen nothing fell,
      Where God's own people dwelt.

9:24   . . . there was hail, and fire flashing continually in the midst of the hail, very heavy hail, such as had never been in all the land of Egypt since it became a nation.

25   The hail struck down everything that was in the field throughout all the land of Egypt, both man and beast; and the hail struck down every plant of the field, and shattered every tree of the field.

26   Only in the land of Goshen, where the people of Israel were, there was no hail.

Exodus

9:35   But Pharaoh's heart would not repent;
           He added sin to sin:
      He was more deaf to God's request
           Than he had ever been.

The Eighth Plague

10:12   The Lord bade Moses take his staff,
           And raise it in his hand
      To make a plague of locusts come,
           And swarm through Pharaoh's
           land.

13   So Moses lifted up his staff,
           And caused a wind to rise;
      And locusts carried by the windstorm
           Thickened Egypt's skies.

9:35   So the heart of Pharaoh was hardened, and he did not let the people of Israel go; as the Lord had spoken through Moses.

10:12   Then the Lord said to Moses, "Stretch out your hand over the land of Egypt for the locusts, that they may come upon the land of Egypt, and eat every plant in the land, all that the hail has left."

13   So Moses stretched forth his rod over the land of Egypt, and the Lord brought an east wind upon the land all that day and all that night; and when it was morning the east wind brought the locusts.

Exodus
10:14   And locusts settled ev'rywhere—
On field, on hill and shore;
No living man had ever seen
Such multitudes before.

And none to come will ever see
In Egypt such a mass,
15   For locusts covered all the earth,
Consuming leaves and grass.

So only shrubs, and fruitless trees,
And barren ground were seen,
For locusts ate the grass and herbs,
And all that had been green.

10:14   And the locusts came up over all the land of
Egypt, and settled on the whole country of
Egypt, such a dense swarm of locusts as had
never been before, nor ever shall be again.
15   For they covered the face of the whole land,
so that the land was darkened, and they ate all
the plants in the land and all the fruit of the
trees which the hail had left; not a green thing
remained, neither tree nor plant of the field,
through all the land of Egypt.

Exodus

10:16 But seeing this the Pharaoh quickly
    Summoned Moses in.
     "I know I wronged your God," he
     said,
      "And recognize my sin;

17 "And I have wronged your people too,
    So ask your God, and pray,
     That he forgive the Pharaoh's sin,
      And take this plague away."

18 So Moses said to God, "The king
    Repents that he has sinned."
19   The Lord God answered Moses'
     prayer,
     And sent a mighty wind

10:16 Then Pharaoh called Moses and Aaron in haste, and said, "I have sinned against the Lord your God, and against you.

17 Now therefore, forgive my sin, I pray you, only this once, and entreat the Lord your God only to remove this death from me."

18 So he went out from Pharaoh and entreated the Lord.

19 And the Lord turned a very strong west wind . . .

Exodus

10:19   That swept the multitude of locusts
           To the ocean floor.
      And all the locusts drowned that day,
           And plagued the land no more.

20   But Pharaoh's will grew iron-clad;
           His heart grew cold as ice;
      He still refused to let them go
           To offer sacrifice.

The Ninth Plague

21   The Lord told Moses, "Take your staff,
           And elevate your hand,
      And I will bring a velvet darkness
           Down upon the land."

10:19   . . . which lifted the locusts and drove them into the Red Sea; not a single locust was left in all the country of Egypt.

20   But the Lord hardened Pharaoh's heart, and he did not let the children of Israel go.

21   Then the Lord said to Moses, "Stretch out your hand toward heaven that there may be darkness over the land of Egypt, a darkness to be felt."

Exodus

10:22   When Moses, therefore, took his staff,
                 And raised his hand on high,
            A darkness thick enough to feel
                 Descended from the sky.

   23   For three full days not one of them
                 Could see another's face;
            So black the darkness that they feared
                 To move from place to place.

            This dark persisted in the land,
                 Remaining day and night,
            But wheresoever Hebrews dwelt,
                 In that place there was light.

10:22   So Moses stretched out his hand toward
            heaven, and there was thick darkness in all
            the land of Egypt three days;

   23   they did not see one another, nor did any rise
            from his place for three days; but all the
            people of Israel had light where they dwelt.

Exodus

10:24 So Pharaoh summoned Moses, saying,
      "Now I change my mind:
  I'll let you go to sacrifice,
      But leave your flocks behind."

25 But Moses told the Pharaoh that
      He asked too great a price,
  For God would have them bring the
        victims
      For the sacrifice.

27 But Pharaoh's anger was aroused—
      He would not have it so:
  And once again he had his way,
      And would not let them go.

10:24 Then Pharaoh called Moses, and said, "Go, serve the Lord; your children also may go with you; only let your flocks and your herds remain behind."

25 But Moses said, "You must also let us have sacrifices and burnt offerings, that we may sacrifice to the Lord our God.

27 But the Lord hardened Pharaoh's heart, and he would not let them go.

Exodus

The Tenth Plague

11:1   The Lord God said to Moses, "I
        Intend to strike once more,
    But this time I will strike them
        More severely than before:

    "So fierce will be the plague I send,
        So serious the blow
    That Pharaoh's heart will be disposed
        To let my people go."

3   Now, Moses was respected there,
        So entered Pharaoh's court,
4   And said, "The God of Israel
        Sends Pharaoh this report:

11:1   The Lord said to Moses, "Yet one plague more
I will bring upon Pharaoh and upon Egypt;
afterwards he will let you go hence; when he
lets you go he will drive you away completely.

3   And the Lord gave the people favor in the
sight of the Egyptians. Moreover, the man of
Moses was very great in the land of Egypt, in
the sight of Pharaoh's servants and in the sight
of the people.

4   And Moses said, "Thus says the Lord: . . .

Exodus
11:4   " 'I'll make my way through Egypt
                In the middle of the night,
            And visit all the homes of Egypt
                With this fatal plight:

5   'Whatever first-born is among you,
                I intend to kill—
            Your own son, Pharaoh, and the sons
                Of handmaids at your mill.' "

        But Pharaoh, angered by the fact
                That God had spoken so,
10   Sent Moses out, and still refused
                To let his people go.

11:4   " '. . . About midnight I will go forth in the
        midst of Egypt;
5   and all the first-born in the land of Egypt shall
        die, from the first-born of Pharaoh who sits
        upon his throne, even to the first-born of the
        maidservant who is behind the mill; and all
        the first-born of the cattle." '
10   . . . and the Lord hardened Pharaoh's heart,
        and he did not let the people of Israel go out
        of his land.

Exodus
12:29 And so at midnight God slew all the
      First-born of the land:
    The Pharaoh's son, the slave girl's
      child,
      Were victims of his hand.

30 All Egypt woke, and in her streets
      Arose a cry of dread—
    In ev'ry house throughout the land,
      The first-born man lay dead.

31 And Pharaoh, calling Moses in
      Before it yet was dawn,
32   Said, "Take your people and your
      flocks,
      Relieve me, and be gone!"

12:29 At midnight the Lord smote all the first-born in the land of Egypt, from the first-born of the Pharaoh who sat on his throne to the first-born of the captive who was in the dungeon, and all the first-born of the cattle.

30 And Pharaoh rose up in the night, he, and all his servants, and all the Egyptians; and there was a great cry in Egypt, for there was not a house where one was not dead.

31 And he summoned Moses and Aaron by night, and said, "Rise up, go forth from among my people, both you and the people of Israel; and go, serve the Lord as you have said.

32 Take your flocks and your herds, as you have said, and be gone; and bless me also!"

Genesis

12:33   So, too, the people pressed the Jews,
         And urged them on their way,
      And begged them, "Leave our country soon,
         Lest we should die today."

12:33   And the Egyptians were urgent with the people, to send them out of the land in haste; for they said, "We are all dead men."

Meditation
drawn from
Psalm 105

Even though Israel went down on her
Knees in Egypt; even though she settled
On the land of Cham, nevertheless:

The Lord increased her number and even
Overcame the odds against her, while the foe
Oppressed her by lying through his teeth.

The Lord had saved an irony or ten,
When it came time to summon Moses
And awaken Aaron to wonder at their
New assignments:

He closed his eyes on Egypt, and a terrible
Darkness covered the land: a darkness invisibly
      thick,
Which Egyptian seers could not see through.
And he clotted their rivers and streams,
Until fish slowed glaze-eyed in the red slush,
      belly-up.
What followed was an exodus of frogs,
Leaping for the land, landing in great heaps,
Creeping through the land,
Crawling in and out of all the best-made beds.

God spoke the word, and flies of every size
(And gnats too small to see) were all at once
      released
On a flying spree over Egypt, darkening the
Skies, and leaving in their wake some horrible,
Relentless sleeping sickness.

Again God spoke: and locusts clustered at his
      word.
In diving droves they arrived in Egypt's skies,
Voracious hordes of dislocated locusts,
Stripping every branch they landed on
Of every shade of green,
Devouring every hope of harvest,
And leaving all Egyptian orchards
Blanched, from north to south.

But then the hand of God pressed down on Israel's
      oppressors.
So severely fell his sword upon the first-born of
      the land,
That Egypt lost the heart of its youth,
And Israel escaped from bondage: free at last
To go with gold and silver for the journey.
No Egyptian delayed them any longer, but rather
Many lined the streets to cheer their exodus,
So glad were they to see them gone.

Ballad VI

The Exodus

from the
Book of Exodus
Chapters 12–14

The Exodus

Exodus

12:37   And so the Israelites set out,
          And brought their goods along,
    They marched, proceeding to the
          north,
          Six hundred thousand strong.

40   Four hundred thirty years ago
          They had begun their stay,
41   And now their legions left the land
          Within a single day.

So thus the people made their exit:
          Pharaoh set them free;
13:18   The Lord God led them to the desert,
          Bordering the sea.

12:37   And the people of Israel journeyed from Rameses to Succoth, about six hundred thousand men on foot, besides women and children.

40   The time that the people of Israel dwelt in Egypt was four hundred and thirty years.

41   And at the end of four hundred and thirty years, on that very day, all the hosts of the Lord went out from the land of Egypt.

13:18   But God led the people round by way of the wilderness toward the Red Sea.

Exodus

13:21   And God went on before the people,
        Pointing out the way:
    A shaft of fire to lead by night,
        A cloud to lead by day.

14:5   Now when the news of their escape
        Had reached the Pharaoh's men,
    The Pharaoh grew disconsolate,
        And changed his mind again:

    He grew impatient with himself,
        And learned the Hebrews' route,
6   And, harnessing his chariot,
        He followed in pursuit.

13:21   And the Lord went before them by day in a pillar of cloud to lead them along the way, and by night in a pillar of fire to give them light . . .

14:15   When the king of Egypt was told that the people had fled, the mind of Pharaoh and his servants was changed toward the people, and they said, "What is this we have done, that we have let Israel go from serving us?"

6   So he made ready his chariot and took his army with him . . .

Exodus

14:7 He chose six hundred chariots,
    The best that could be found,
    And chose six hundred army captains,
    Egypt's most renowned.

9 They found the fugitives encamped,
    But hemmed in by the sea;
10   The Hebrews saw the Pharaoh's men,
    And feared exceedingly.

12 So crying out to Moses, then,
    They blamed him for their fear:
    "Much better to be slaves in Egypt,
    Than to die out here."

14:7 . . . and took six hundred picked chariots and all the other chariots of Egypt with officers over all of them.

9 The Egyptians pursued them, all Pharaoh's horses and chariots . . . and overtook them encamped at the sea . . .

10 When Pharaoh drew near . . . the people of Israel cried out to the Lord; and they said to Moses . . .

12 ". . . it would have been better for us to serve the Egyptians than to die in the wilderness."

Exodus

14:13   But Moses stood apart and said,
           "My children, hold your peace:
14   The Lord intends to fight for you;
           His might will never cease."

15   The Lord God said to Moses:
           "Moses, you have called on me—
    So tell my chosen people to march
        Onward to the sea;

16   "But lift your hand, stretch forth your rod,
           Divide the sea in two,
    And I will dry the muddy ground,
        And lead my people through!"

14:13   And Moses said to the people, "Fear not, stand firm, and see the salvation of the Lord, which he will work for you today . . .

14   The Lord will fight for you and you have only to be still."

15   The Lord said to Moses, "Why do you cry to me? Tell the people of Israel to go forward.

16   Lift up your rod, and stretch out your hand over the sea and divide it, that the people of Israel may go on dry ground through the sea."

Exodus

14:21   When Moses lifted up his hand,
                 The waters opened wide,
          And all night long a strong wind blew;
                 The muddy bed was dried.

22   And so the people marched on through:
                 The waters had been cleft,
          And walls of water towered on
                 Their right and on their left.

23   And Egypt's army followed them,
                 And all of Pharaoh's men,
26   But God bade Moses lift his hand,
                 And close the sea again.

14:21   Then Moses stretched out his hand over the sea; and the Lord drove the sea back by a strong east wind all night, and made the sea dry land, and the waters were divided.

22   And the people of Israel went into the midst of sea on dry ground, the waters being a wall to them on their right hand and on their left.

23   The Egyptians pursued, and went in after them into the midst of the sea, all Pharaoh's horses, his chariots, and his horsemen.

26   Then the Lord said to Moses, "Stretch out your hand over the sea, that the water may come back upon the Egyptians . . . "

Exodus

14:27   So Moses stood above the sea,
          And lifted up his hand;
        The Lord God shut the sea again,
          And drowned the Pharaoh's band.

28   The sea destroyed the chariots,
          And all that they contained,
       And of the army Pharaoh sent,
          Not one of them remained.

29   But God's own people marched upon
          The clay that had been dried—
       The sea remained apart for them,
          With walls on either side.

14:27   So Moses stretched forth his hand over the sea, and the sea returned to its wonted flow when the morning appeared; and the Egyptians fled into it, and the Lord routed the Egyptians in the midst of the sea.

28   The waters returned and covered the chariots and the horsemen and all the host of Pharaoh that had followed them into the sea; not so much as one of them remained.

29   But the people of Israel walked on dry ground through the sea, the waters being a wall to them on their right hand and on their left.

Exodus

14:30   This day their God had rescued them;
         Their freedom was restored,
  31   And all the people recognized
         The power of the Lord,

For all the spoils of the army
         Showed what God could do,
So they believed in him that day,
         And rev'renced Moses, too.

14:30   Thus the Lord saved Israel that day from the hand of the Egyptians; and Israel saw the Egyptians dead upon the seashore.

31   And Israel saw the great work which the Lord did against the Egyptians, and the people feared the Lord; and they believed in the Lord and in his servant Moses.

Meditation drawn from Psalm 114

On the day that Israel marched out from Egypt—
When the entire house of Jacob moved away from
    a strange people,
An inhospitable nation, whose music made no
    sense—
What a time that was:
Judah became the place where God would come to
    stay,
Israel the people among whom God would make
    his home.

The sea no sooner saw this coming
Than it caved in and fled from their approach,
The River Jordan turned around and ran.
Huge mountains lost their composure on that day,
And skipped around, like absent-minded goats.
Rolling foothills fell quickly into step and
    stumbled close behind,
Like little lambs.

What so alarmed you, Mighty Sea, that you
       stopped your roaring waves?
And you, River Jordan, what shook you so that
       you turned around
And ran in the wrong direction?
You Mighty Mountains: what did it take to take
       you by surprise,
Like startled goats? Staid foothills, what moved
       you to behave
So sheepishly?

O Planet Earth: Prepare to quake at God's
       approach,
To tremble when you find Him living with his
       people.
He is the One in whose wake your hardest flint
       will flow like lava,
Your molten rock run cold like water in your
       veins. Amen.

Ballad VII

The Ten Commandments

from the
Book of Exodus
Chapters 19–20

The Ten Commandments

Exodus
19:16 Now on the third day of their fast,
    The morn began to dawn,
And thunder pealed, and shook the
    mountain;
    Lightning flashed and shone.

And over Sinai's trembling peak
    The sun began to rise,
But fog persisted, and there was
    A mist throughout the skies.

And suddenly a trumpet blast
    Came ringing through the air,
Whose detonation scattered wide
    The people who were there.

19:16   On the morning of the third day there were thunders and lightnings, and a thick cloud upon the mountain, and a very loud trumpet blast, so that all the people who were in the camp trembled.

115

Exodus

19:17   But Moses brought them from the camp,
            That they might meet the Lord,
      So they approached the Holy Mount
            Where flames and cinders roared.

18   The whole of Sinai was encompassed
            In a smoky cloud—
      When God came down, surrounded by
            A bright and flaming shroud.

19   And louder still the trumpet's blast
            Came piercing through the sky,
      And Moses knelt, and spoke to God,
            And all heard God's reply:

19:17   Then Moses brought the people out of the camp to meet God; and they took their stand at the foot of the mountain.

18   And Mount Sinai was wrapped in smoke, because the Lord descended upon it in fire; and the smoke of it went up like the smoke of a kiln, and the whole mountain quaked greatly.

19   And as the sound of the trumpet grew louder and louder, Moses spoke, and God answered him in thunder.

Exodus

20:2　　"I am the Lord thy God," he said,
　　　　　　　"And I have set thee free,
　　　　　And I have rescued thee from Egypt,
　　　　　　　Out of slavery.

　3　　"And thou shalt carve no images
　4　　　　　From earth or from above,
　5　　　　For I, the Lord thy God, am very
　　　　　　　Jealous in my love.

　　　　"For I will strike the infidels
　　　　　　　Who worship calves of gold;
　6　　　　But keep my laws, and mercy shall be
　　　　　　　Thine a thousandfold.

————————————

20:2　　"I am the Lord your God, who brought you
　　　　out of the land of Egypt, out of the house of
　　　　bondage.

　3　　You shall have no other gods before me.

　4　　You shall not make for yourself a graven im-
　　　　age, or any likeness of anything that is in
　　　　heaven above, or that is in the earth beneath,
　　　　or that is in the water under the earth;

　5　　you shall not bow down to them or serve
　　　　them; for I the Lord your God am a jealous
　　　　God . . .

　6　　but showing steadfast love to thousands of
　　　　those who love me and keep my command-
　　　　ments.

Exodus

20:7   "I am the Lord thy only God;
         None other shalt thou claim,
      Nor shalt thou utter blasphemies
         Against my sacred name.

    "Thou shalt not speak the name of God
         In anger or in jest,
      For such a man that does this
         Puts my mercy to the test.

8   "Remember keep the Sabbath Day,
         And put thy work aside;
9   Six days there are for labor,
10   But this day is sanctified.

20:7   "You shall not take the name of the Lord your God in vain; for the Lord will not hold him guiltless who takes his name in vain.

8   Remember the sabbath day, to keep it holy.

9   Six days you shall labor, and do all your work;

10   but the seventh day is a sabbath to the Lord your God . . .

Exodus

20:12   "Obey thy parents, honor them,
             And thou shalt surely live
        For length of days upon the land,
             Which only God can give.

13   "Thou shalt not kill thy fellow man,
             Nor plot against his life,
14   Nor shalt thou dare commit adult'ry
             With another's wife.

15   "Thou shalt not take another's goods,
             Nor keep what is not thine,
16   Nor shalt thou bear false witness,
             By an action or a sign.

20:12   "Honor your father and your mother, that your days may be long in the land which the Lord your God gives you.

13   "You shall not kill.

14   "You shall not commit adultery.

15   "You shall not steal.

16   "You shall not bear false witness against your neighbor.

119

Exodus

20:17 "Thou shalt not covet anything
        Thy neighbor calls his own,
    Nor have desire for his wife,
        For she is his alone."

18 And all the people stood enthralled,
        As thunder rolled and crashed;
    The trumpet sounded once again,
        And streaks of lightning flashed.

The mountain was enwreathed by smoke
        That belched forth from inside,
    And all the people kept their
        distance,
        Awed and terrified.

20:17 "You shall not covet your neighbor's house; you shall not covet your neighbor's wife, or his manservant, or his maidservant, or his ox, or his ass, or anything that is your neighbor's."

18 Now when all the people perceived the thunderings and the lightnings and the sound of the trumpet and the mountain smoking, the people were afraid and trembled; and they stood afar off . . .

Exodus

20:19   They shouted, "Tell us his command,
              And we shall all comply,
          But do not let us hear God speak,
              Or we shall surely die."

20   And Moses said, "Be not afraid,
              For God comes as your friend;
          He urges you to serve him, that your
              Wickedness might end."

21   And Moses climbed the mountaintop,
              Where he had been at first;
          Then evening came, and dark took
              hold,
          And all the crowd dispersed.

20:19 . . . and said to Moses, "You speak to us, and we will hear; but let not God speak to us, lest we die."

20   And Moses said to the people, "Do not fear; for God has come to prove you, and that the fear of him may be before your eyes, that you may not sin."

21   And the people stood afar off, while Moses drew near to the thick darkness where God was.

Meditation
drawn from
Psalm 119

Happiness comes as a gift
To those who will drop their foot-dragging habit,
To find there is balance aplenty
In the equilibrium of law.
Happy indeed are the sure-footed,
Who abandon the sadness of straddling.

Notice the wholeness of heart
Of those who leap in order to look:
Of those who inquire after the ways of God,
To find what He might have in mind for them.

Lord, you have been revealing
Your highest hopes in our regard all along:
In a way that we can understand,
In a way that we can learn from,
In a way that we can go along with.

Teach me not to lean away from your law,
But to learn step by blessed step
To understand your best intentions.
In any event
I will no longer need to stray,
Or daily hide, an aimless fugitive,
Afraid of being discovered and forever shamed,
Worried sick and ill-at-ease
Over outcomes and eventualities.

At each turning I will learn
That your decrees, thank God,
Are amazing clues along the way,
Free for the reading. I can move
Through this life newly in the mood to listen
To your sound advice, which speaks to me
Of promise and reliability, so far
As I can ascertain. All is founded,
Please God, on your enduring strength: on
Your abiding inability to lie to me,
Or ever to abandon me utterly
To my own devices. Amen.